PUR... ...for
EVERYDAY
LIVING

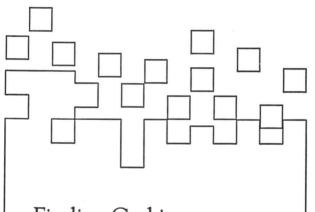

Finding God in
Your Everyday Life

CRISWELL FREEMAN

PURPOSE *for* EVERYDAY LIVING

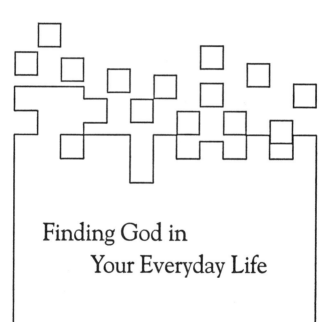

Finding God in
Your Everyday Life

The quoted ideas expressed in this book (but not scripture verses) are not, in all cases, exact quotations, as some have been edited for clarity and brevity. In all cases, the author has attempted to maintain the speaker's original intent. In some cases, quoted material for this book was obtained from secondary sources, primarily print media. While every effort was made to ensure the accuracy of these sources, the accuracy cannot be guaranteed. For additions, deletions, corrections or clarifications in future editions of this text, please contact Paul Shepherd, Editor in Chief for Elm Hill Books.
Email pshepherd@elmhillbooks.com

Products from Elm Hill Books may be purchased in bulk for educational, business, fundraising, or sales promotional use. For information, please email SpecialMarkets@ThomasNelson.com.

Scripture quotations marked (NKJV) are taken from *The Holy Bible*: New King James Version (NKJV). Copyright © 1979, 1980, 1982 by Thomas Nelson, Inc. Used by permission. All rights reserved.

Cover Design by Karen Phillips
Page Layout by Bart Dawson

Purpose for Everyday Living ISBN 1-4041-8538-0

TABLE OF CONTENTS

God has a plan for everything, including you. As a part of that plan, He intends you experience abundance and joy in this life, *and* throughout all eternity. But perhaps *your* vision of what God intends for your life is not quite as clear as you would like. If so, this book is intended to help.

The ideas on these pages are intended as tools to assist you in discovering the unfolding plans and purposes God has in store for you. This text does not attempt to answer every question concerning your particular situation; instead, it gives you Biblically-based, time-tested directions for the journey ahead.

If you sincerely seek God's guidance for your life, He will give it. But He will make His revelations known to you in a way and in a time of *His* choosing, not yours. So, if you're sincerely seeking to know God's will for your life, don't be worried if you haven't yet received a "final" answer. The final answer, of course, will come not in this world, but in the next.

If you've encountered circumstances you don't fully understand, don't be discouraged. Instead of fretting about the future, open your heart to God in the present moment. Listen to Him, and do the work He has placed before you. Then, rest assured, if you genuinely trust God and accept the salvation of His only begotten Son, God's plans for you will be as perfect as His love.

THE POWER
OF
PURPOSE

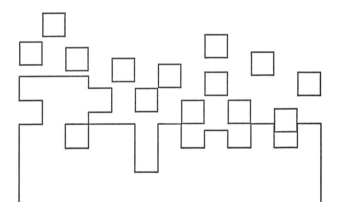

You will show me the path of life;
In Your presence is fullness of joy;
At Your right hand are pleasures
forevermore.
Psalm 16:11 NKJV

L ife is best lived on purpose, not by accident: the sooner we discover what God intends for us to do with our lives, the better. But God's purposes aren't always clear to us. Sometimes we wander aimlessly in a wilderness of our own making. Sometimes we struggle mightily against God, in a vain effort to find success and happiness through our own means, not His.

Whenever we struggle against God's plans, we suffer. When we resist God's calling, our efforts bear little fruit. Our best strategy, therefore, is to seek God's wisdom and follow Him wherever He chooses to lead. When we do so, we are blessed.

When we align ourselves with God's purposes, we avail ourselves of His power and His peace. But how can we know precisely what God's intentions are? The answer, of course, is that even the most well-intentioned believers face periods of uncertainty and doubt about the direction of their lives. So, too, will you.

When you arrive at one of life's inevitable crossroads, that is precisely the moment when you should turn your thoughts and prayers toward God. When you do, He will make Himself known to you in a time and manner of His choosing.

Are you earnestly seeking to discern God's purpose for your life? If so, these pages are intended as a reminder of several important facts: 1. God has a plan for your life; 2. If you seek that plan sincerely and prayerfully, you will find it; 3. When you discover God's purpose for your life, you will experience abundance, peace, joy, and power—God's power—the only power that really matters.

Continually restate to yourself
what the purpose of your life is.
Oswald Chambers

The study of inspired Scripture is
the chief way of finding our duty.
St. Basil the Great

We must focus on prayer as the main thrust to
accomplish God's will and purpose on earth.
The forces against us have never been greater,
and this is the only way we can release
God's power to become victorious.
John Maxwell

The born-again Christian sees life not
as a blurred, confused, meaningless mass,
but as something planned and purposeful.
Billy Graham

If the Lord calls you, He will equip you for
the task He wants you to fulfill.
Warren Wiersbe

When God is involved, anything can happen.
Be open and stay that way. God has
a beautiful way of bringing good vibrations
out of broken chords.
Charles Swindoll

Even when we cannot see the why
and wherefore of God's dealings, we know
that there is love in and behind them,
so we can rejoice always.

J. I. Packer

Every person's life is a plan of God.

Horace Bushnell

Have I today done anything to fulfil
the purpose for which Thou didst
cause me to be born?

John Baillie

We are all pencils in
the hand of God.

—

Mother Teresa

Nothing in this world is without meaning.
A. W. Tozer

More people fail from lack of purpose
than lack of talent.
Billy Sunday

When I stand before God at the end of my life,
I would hope that I would not have
a single bit of talent left and could say,
"I used everything you gave me."
Erma Bombeck

Think of these things, whence you came,
where you are going,
and to whom you must account.
Ben Franklin

Fear not that thy life shall
come to an end, but rather
fear that it shall
never have a beginning.
—

Cardinal Newman

Open Yourself Up To God

Perhaps you have been overly anxious to impose your own plans upon the world. If so, it's time to open yourself up to God. If you have been struggling against God's will for your life, you have invited unwelcome consequences into your own life *and* into the lives of your loved ones. A far better strategy is to consult God earnestly and consistently *before* you embark upon the next stage of your life's journey.

FINDING GOD'S PURPOSE

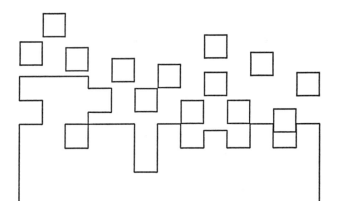

*And we know that all things work together
for good to those who love God,
to those who are the called
according to His purpose.*
Romans 8:28 NKJV

"What did God put me here to do?" If you're like most people, you've asked yourself that on many occasions. Perhaps you have pondered over your future, uncertain of your plans, unsure of your next step. But even if *you* don't have a clear plan for the next step of your life's journey, you may rest assured *God* does.

God has a plan for the universe, and He has a plan for you. He understands that plan as thoroughly and completely as He knows you. If you seek God's will earnestly and prayerfully, He will make His plans known to you in His own time and in His own way.

Do you sincerely seek to discover God's purpose for your life? If so, you must first be willing to live in accordance with His commandments. You must also study God's Word, and be watchful for His signs. Finally, you should open yourself up to the Creator every day—beginning with this one. You must have faith He will soon reveal His plans to you.

Perhaps your vision of God's purpose for your life has been clouded by a wish list you have expected God to dutifully fulfill. Perhaps, you have fervently hoped God would create a world that unfolds according to *your* wishes, not His. If so, you have experienced more disappointment than satisfaction, and more frustration than peace. A better strategy is to conform *your* will to God's (not to struggle vainly in an attempt to conform *His* will to yours).

Sometimes God's plans and purposes may seem unmistakably clear to you. If so, push ahead. At other times, He may lead you through the wilderness, before He directs you to the Promised Land. Be patient. Keep seeking His will for your life. When you do, you'll be amazed at the marvelous things an all-powerful, all-knowing God can do.

Aim at Heaven
and you will get earth
"thrown in"; aim at earth
and you will get neither.
—
C. S. Lewis

Unless the LORD builds the house,
they labor in vain who build it;
unless the LORD guards the city,
the watchman stays awake in vain.
Psalm 127:1 NKJV

Their distress is due entirely to their
deliberate determination to use themselves
for a purpose other than God's.
Oswald Chambers

Without God, life has no purpose,
and without purpose, life has no meaning.
Rick Warren

Live out your life in
its full meaning.
It is God's life.
—

Josiah Royce

Live your life while you have it.
Life is a splendid gift—there is nothing
small about it.
Florence Nightingale

*For I know the thoughts that I think
toward you, says the LORD, thoughts of peace
and not of evil, to give you a future and a hope.*
Jeremiah 29:11 NKJV

You were made by God and for God—
and until you understand that,
life will not make sense.
Rick Warren

Life is God's novel.
Let him write it.

—

Isaac Bashevis Singer

A man's heart plans his way,
But the LORD directs his steps.
Proverbs 16:9 NKJV

The study of inspired Scripture is
the chief way of finding our duty.
St. Basil the Great

If God declares what it means to be human,
then our lives are not the meaningless
collections of unrelated events
they so often appear to be.
Stanley Grenz

Focus on Purposes, Not Wishes

Ask yourself this question: "Is it my wish list or God's?" If you're struggling mightily to keep up with the Jones, you may be struggling in vain. But if you set your personal wish list aside and instead seek God's purposes for your life, He will lead you in the direction you should go. Never allow greed, fear, selfishness, or pride to separate you from the will of God. Seek His kingdom first, and then have faith He will provide all the things that you *need*, even if He does not grant all the things you *want*.

DAILY PRAYER
AND
MEDITATION

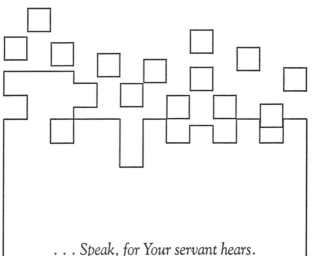

. . . *Speak, for Your servant hears.*
1 Samuel 3:10 NKJV

Your search to discover God's purpose for your life is not a destination; it is a journey that unfolds day by day. And that is exactly how often you should seek direction from your Creator: one day at a time, each day followed by the next, without exception.

Daily prayer and meditation are a matter of will and habit. You must willingly organize your time by carving out quiet moments with God. You must form the habit of daily worship. When you do, you'll discover no time is more precious than the silent moments you spend with your Heavenly Father.

God promises the prayers of righteous men and women can accomplish great things. God promises He answers prayer (although *His* answers are not always in accordance with *our* desires). God invites us to be still and feel His presence. So pray. Start praying before the sun comes up. Keep praying until you fall off to sleep at night. Pray about matters great and small; and be watchful for the answers God most assuredly sends your way.

Is prayer an integral part of your daily life, or is it a hit-or-miss routine? Do you "pray without ceasing," or is your prayer life an afterthought? Do you regularly pray in the solitude of the early morning darkness, or do you bow your head only when others are watching?

The quality of your spiritual life will be in direct proportion to the quality of your prayer life. Prayer changes things, and it changes you. Today, instead of turning things over in your mind, turn them over to God in prayer. Instead of worrying about your next decision, ask God to lead the way. Don't limit your prayers to meals or to bedtime; pray constantly. God is listening. He wants to hear from you. You most certainly need to hear from Him.

Prayer keeps us in constant communion
with God, which is the goal of
our entire believing lives.
Beth Moore

When we pray, we have linked ourselves
with Divine purposes, and we therefore
have Divine power at our disposal
for human living.
E. Stanley Jones

True prayer is measured by weight,
not by length. A single groan before
God may have more fullness of prayer
in it than a fine oration of great length.
C. H. Spurgeon

Leadership requires vision, and whence will
vision come except from hours spent in
the presence of God in humble
and fervent prayer?
A. W. Tozer

Don't pray when you feel like it;
make an appointment
with the King and keep it.
Corrie ten Boom

History has been changed time after time
because of prayer. I tell you, history could be
changed again if people went to their
knees in believing prayer.
Billy Graham

The more a person bows his knee before God,
the straighter he stands before men.
Anonymous

The only way to pray is to pray;
and the way to pray well is to pray much.
Henri Nouwen

Every work of God can be traced
to some kneeling form.
D. L. Moody

The purpose of all prayer is
to find God's will
and to make that will
our prayer.
—

Catherine Marshall

God shapes the world by prayer.
The more praying there is in the world,
the better the world will be,
and the mightier will be
the forces against evil.
E. M. Bounds

Prayer connects us with
God's limitless potential.
Henry Blackaby

Even more than we long to be heard,
God desires to listen.
Angela Thomas

Prayer is the deliberate
and persevering action of
the soul. It is true and
enduring, and full of grace.
Prayer fastens the soul to
God and makes it one
with God's will.

—

Juliana of Norwich

Take Full Advantage of The Morning

If you're staying up late and sleeping through the early morning hours, perhaps it's time to rearrange your schedule. The French dramatist *Jean Giraudoux* observed, "Sadness flies on the wings of the morning, and out of the heart of darkness comes the light." Each new dawn breaks over a world filled to the brim with possibilities. If your work schedule requires you to sleep through the early morning hours, at least you'll have a good reason for missing out on God's early-morning fireworks. But if you're staying up in order to watch one more late-night rerun, do yourself a favor: go to bed. As Ben Franklin correctly observed, "The early morning hath gold in its mouth."

FINDING
PURPOSE
AT HOME

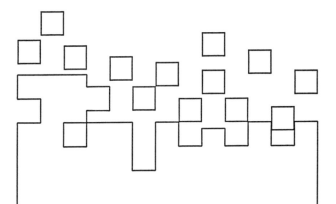

*. . . choose for yourselves this day
whom you will serve . . . as for me
and my house, we will serve the LORD.*
Joshua 24:15 NKJV

As you consider God's purpose for your own life, you must also consider how your plans will effect the most important people God has entrusted to your care: your loved ones.

A loving family is a treasure from God. If you happen to be a member of a close knit, supportive clan, offer a word of thanks to your Creator. He has blessed you with one of His most precious earthly possessions. Your obligation, in response to God's gift, is to treat your family in ways that are consistent with His commandments.

We live in a competitive world, a place where earning a living can be difficult and demanding. As pressures build, we may tend to focus so intently upon our economic concerns, we lose sight, albeit temporarily, of our other, more important needs (one reason why a regular daily devotional time is so important: it offers a dose of perspective).

God intends we honor Him by honoring our families. We honor our families by giving them our love, our support, our advice, our cooperation, and when needed, our discipline. Make no mistake: these matters require significant investments of time.

No family is perfect, and neither is yours. Yet in spite of the inevitable challenges of family life, your clan is God's gift to you. That little band of men, women, kids, and babies comprises a priceless treasure on temporary loan from the Father above. As you prayerfully seek God's direction, remember He has important plans for your home life as well as your professional life. It's up to you to act—and to plan—accordingly.

Disorder in the society is
the result of disorder in the family.
Angela Merici

Homes that are built on anything
other than love are bound to crumble.
Billy Graham

The family that prays together, stays together.
Anonymous

Happiness is to be found only in
the home where God is loved and honored,
where each one loves, and helps,
and cares for the others.

St. Theophane Venard

Whole-life stewardship means putting
the purposes of God at the very center
of our lives and families.

Tom Sine

The strength of a nation is derived
from the integrity of its homes.

Confucius

We must strengthen our
commitment to model strong
families ourselves, to live by
godly priorities in a culture
where self so often supersedes
commitment to others.
And, as we not only model
but assertively reach out to help
others, we must realize that
even huge societal problems are
solved one person at a time.
—

Chuck Colson

Money can build or buy a house.
Add love to that, and you have a home.
Add God to that, and you have a temple.
You have "a little colony of
the kingdom of heaven."
Anne Ortland

Creating a warm, caring, supportive,
encouraging environment is probably
the most important thing
you can do for your family.
Stephen Covey

The crown of the home is godliness.
Henry Van Dyke

The most effective thing
we can do for our children and
families is to pray for them.
—
Anthony Evans

A home is a place where we find direction.
Gigi Graham Tchividjian

The only true source of meaning in life is found
in love for God and his son Jesus Christ,
and love for mankind,
beginning with our own families.
James Dobson

My primary role is not to be the boss
and just look good, but to be a servant leader
who enables and enhances my family
to be their best.
Tim Hansel

Taking Time and Making Time for Family

How much time should you dedicate to your family? The answer is straightforward: You should invest large *quantities* of *high-quality* time in caring for your clan. As you nurture your loved ones, you should do your very best to ensure God remains squarely at the center of your family's life. When you do, He will bless you—and yours—in ways you could have scarcely imagined.

FINDING PURPOSE IN THE WORKPLACE

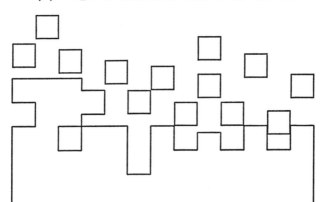

*And whatever you do, do it heartily,
as to the Lord and not to men.*
Colossians 3:23 NKJV

6-17-07

If you've found work you love, and if, through your efforts, you help make the world a better place, consider yourself doubly blessed. But if you're dissatisfied with your employment, or if you feel your professional life is not pleasing to God, there's only one thing to do: you must keep searching.

Perhaps you've been searching for work that is *pleasing to other people*. Perhaps you find yourself struggling in a job that is *not suited to your skills*. In either case, you must remember God made you exactly as you are. He did so for a very good reason: *His* reason. Therefore, you must glorify God by honoring the talents *He gave you*, not the talents *you wish* He had given you.

When you discover the work for which God created you, you'll be productive and inspired. But until you find that work, you'll have trouble generating the enthusiasm. Unfortunately, too many of us have become intensely passionate about things that improve neither the world nor ourselves. We fritter away precious hours in front of the television. We fall deeply in love with alcohol, drugs, gambling, or other addictive behaviors that leave little time, or energy, for anything else.

Have you found work about which you are passionate? Have you discovered a vocation that inspires you to arrive at the office ten minutes early rather than ten minutes late? Does your work help to create a better world *and* a better you? If the answer to these questions is yes, consider yourself both fortunate and wise. But if the dream of meaningful work remains elusive, keep searching—and praying—until you find it.

Thank God every morning when you get up
that you have something which must be done,
whether you like it or not. Work breeds
a hundred virtues that idleness never knows.
Charles Kingsley

Work is such a beautiful and helpful thing,
and independence so delightful that I wonder
why there are any lazy people in the world.
Louisa May Alcott

The road to happiness lies in two simple
principles: find what it is that interests you
and that you can do well, and when you find it,
put your whole soul into it, every bit of energy
and ambition and natural ability you have.
John D. Rockefeller III

Think enthusiastically about everything,
especially your work.
Norman Vincent Peale

Laziness may appear attractive,
but work gives satisfaction.
Anne Frank

What a great prize it is:
the chance to work hard
at work worth doing.
Theodore Roosevelt

To love what you do and feel that it matters—
how could anything be more fun?
Katherine Graham

I seem to have been led, little by little,
toward my work; and I believe that
the same fact will appear in the life of anyone
who will cultivate such powers as God has given
him and then go on, bravely, quietly,
but persistently, doing such work
as comes to his hands.
Fanny Crosby

Each man has his own vocation;
his talent is his call. There is one direction in
which all space is open to him.
Ralph Waldo Emerson

*Whatever your hand finds to do,
do it with your might.*
Ecclesiastes 9:10 NKJV

Work joyfully and peacefully, knowing that
right thoughts and right efforts
will inevitably bring about right results.
James Allen

I long to accomplish a great and noble task,
but it is my chief duty to accomplish
small tasks as if they were great and noble.
Helen Keller

Ordinary work, which is what most of us do
most of the time, is ordained by God
every bit as much as is the extraordinary.
Elisabeth Elliot

The best preparation for tomorrow is to do
today's work superbly well.
William Osler

Christians are to "labor," which refers to hard,
manual work. Hard work is honorable.
As Christians we should work hard so that
we will have enough to give to those in need,
not so that we will have more of
what we don't need.
John MacArthur

Hands are made for work,
and the heart is made for God.
Josepha Rossello

The world does not consider
labor a blessing, therefore
it flees and hates it, but
the pious who fear
the Lord labor with
a ready and cheerful heart,
for they know God's command,
and they acknowledge
His calling.

—

Martin Luther

Finding your particular talent or vocation is
the first step in the art of being successful.
Conrad Hilton

Originality and a feeling of one's own dignity
are achieved only through work and struggle.
Fyodor Dostoyevsky

Nobody who ever gave his best regretted it.
George Halas

. . . every work that he began . . .
he did it with all his heart.
So he prospered.
—
2 Chronicles 31:21 NKJV

Don't "Settle" for Less

In terms of a career choice, most people find it is easy to "settle" for a job that is safe and familiar. Don't be like most people. After all, God didn't create you for mediocrity.

If you feel passionately about your work and that you're well suited for the task at hand, say a word of thanks. If on the other hand, you feel underemployed (or if you feel your skills might be better used in another way), ask God for the courage, the perseverance, and the wisdom you need to select a more suitable path.

PRAYING ON PURPOSE FOR PURPOSE

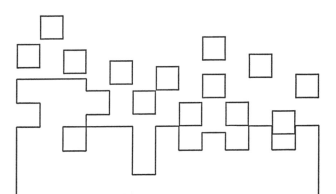

Ask, and it will be given to you;
seek, and you will find;
knock, and the door will be opened to you.
For everyone who asks receives,
he who seeks finds, and to him
who knocks it will be opened.
Matthew 7:7-8 NKJV

Have you fervently asked God for His guidance in every aspect of your life? If so, then you're continually inviting your Creator to reveal Himself in a variety of ways. As a follower of Christ, you must do no less.

Jesus made it clear to His disciples: they should pray always. So should we. Genuine, heartfelt prayer produces powerful changes in us, *and* in our world. When we lift our hearts to our Father in heaven, we open ourselves to a never-ending source of divine wisdom and infinite love.

Do you have questions about your future you simply can't answer? Ask for the guidance of your heavenly Father. Do you sincerely seek to know God's purpose for your life? Then ask Him for direction—and *keep* asking Him every day you live. Whatever your need, no matter how great or small, pray about it, and never lose hope. God is not just near; He is here. He's ready to talk with you—Now!

Some people pray just to pray,
and some people pray
to know God.

—

Andrew Murray

It is in a prayer relationship that
God gives further direction.
Henry Blackaby and Claude King

If you lack knowledge, go to school.
If you lack wisdom, get on your knees.
Vance Havner

All excellence involves discipline
and tenacity of purpose.
John W. Gardner

*Fulfill my joy by
being like-minded,
having the same love,
being of one accord,
of one mind.*
—
Philippians 2:2 NKJV

Prayer is not a lovely sedan for a sightseeing
trip around the city. Prayer is a truck that
goes straight to the warehouse, backs up,
loads, and comes home with the goods.
John R. Rice

Prayer plumes the wings of God's young eaglets
so that they may learn to mount above
the clouds. Prayer brings inner strength to
God's warriors and sends them forth to
spiritual battle with their muscles firm
and their armor in place.
C. H. *Spurgeon*

Prayer is never the least
we can do;
it is always the most!
—
A. W. Tozer

There will be no power in our lives
apart from prayer.
Angela Thomas

Prayer shouldn't be casual or sporadic,
dictated only by the needs of the moment.
Prayer should be as much a apart of
our lives as breathing.
Billy Graham

Never say you will pray about a thing;
pray about it.
Oswald Chambers

Rejoice always, pray without ceasing,
in everything give thanks; for this is
the will of God in Christ Jesus for you.
1 Thessalonians 5:16-18 NKJV

The best way to get on your feet
is to get on your knees.
Anonymous

May He grant you according to
your heart's desire,
and fulfill all your purpose.
Psalm 20:4 NKJV

If God, like a father, denies us what we want
now, it is in order to give us some far better
thing later on. The will of God, we can rest
assured, is invariably a better thing.
Elisabeth Elliot

Sometimes, the Answer Is "No."

God does not answer all of our prayers in the affirmative, nor should He. His job is not to grant all our earthly requests; His job is to offer us eternal salvation (for which we must be forever grateful).

When we are disappointed by the realities of life-here-on-earth, we should remember our prayers are always answered by a sovereign, all-knowing God. We must trust Him, whether He answers "Yes", "No", or "Not yet".

MIDCOURSE CORRECTIONS: WHEN LIFE THROWS YOU A CURVEBALL

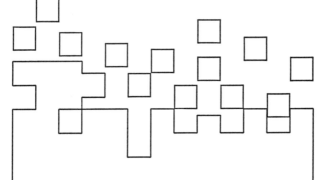

To everything there is a season,
a time for every purpose under heaven.
Ecclesiastes 3:1 NKJV

6-17-07

Our world is in a state of constant change. God is not. At times, the world seems to be trembling beneath our feet. But we can be comforted in the knowledge our Heavenly Father is the rock that cannot be shaken. His Word promises, "I am the LORD, I do not change" (Malachi 3:6 NKJV).

Every day we live, we mortals encounter a multitude of changes—some good, some not so good. On occasion, all of us must endure life-changing personal losses that leave us breathless. When we do, our loving Heavenly Father stands ready to protect us, to comfort us, to guide us, and, in time, to heal us.

Are you facing difficult circumstances, or unwelcome changes? If so, please remember God is far bigger than any problem you may face. Instead of worrying about life's inevitable challenges, put your faith in the Father and His only begotten Son: "Jesus Christ is the same yesterday, today, and forever" (Hebrews 13:8 NKJV). Then, rest assured: It is precisely because your Savior does not change, that you can face your challenges with courage for today and hope for tomorrow.

Are you anxious about situations you cannot control? Take your anxieties to God. Are you troubled? Take your troubles to Him. Does your corner of the world seem to be trembling beneath your feet? Seek protection from the One who cannot be moved. The same God who created the universe will protect you if you ask Him—so ask Him. Then serve Him with willing hands and a trusting heart.

If God has you in the palm of his hand
and your real life is secure in him,
then you can venture forth—into the places
and relationships, the challenges,
the very heart of the storm—
and you will be safe there.
Paula Rinehart

It is well and good if all things change,
Lord, if we are rooted in You.
St. John of the Cross

*Let not your heart be troubled;
you believe in God, believe also in Me.*
John 14:1 NKJV

He who is fretted by
his own failings will not
correct them; all profitable
correction comes from a calm,
peaceful mind.

—

St. Francis of Sales

You cannot step twice in the same river,
for other waters are continually flowing on.
Heraclitus

The only way a person can remain consistent
amid changing circumstances is to change
with them while preserving
the same dominating purpose.
Winston Churchill

We must adjust to changing times
and still hold to unchanging principles.
Jimmy Carter

The secret of a happy life:
Accept change gracefully.
Jimmy Stewart

Change your thoughts,
and you change your world.
Norman Vincent Peale

It is never too late—in fiction
or in life—to revise.
Nancy Thayer

More often than not,
when something looks like
it's the absolute end,
it is really the beginning.
—

Charles Swindoll

God, give us the serenity to accept what
cannot be changed. Give us courage to
change what should be changed. Give us
the wisdom to distinguish one from the other.
Reinhold Niebuhr

For we walk by faith, not by sight.
2 Corinthians 5:7 NKJV

Let nothing disturb you, nothing frighten you;
all things are passing; God never changes.
St. Teresa of Avila

Slowing Down the Merry-go-round

Every major change, whether bad *or* good, puts stress on you and your family. That's why it's sensible to plan things so you don't invite too many changes into your life at once. You will be tempted to do otherwise. Once you land that new job, you'll be sorely tempted to buy the new house and the new car. If you've just gotten married, you'll be tempted to buy everything in sight—while the credit card payments mount. Don't do it! When it comes to making big changes or big purchases, proceed slowly. Otherwise, you may find yourself uncomfortably perched atop a merry-go-round that is much easier to start, than it is to stop.

THE FAITH
TO MOVE
MOUNTAINS

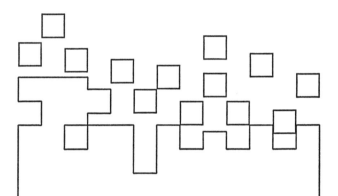

*. . . If you have faith as a mustard seed,
you will say to this mountain,
'Move from here to there,' and it will move;
and nothing will be impossible for you.*
Matthew 17:20 NKJV

Every life—including yours—is a series of successes and failures, celebrations and disappointments, joys and sorrows. Every step of the way, through every triumph and tragedy, God will stand by your side and strengthen you—if you have faith in Him. Jesus taught his disciples that if they had faith, they could move mountains. You can too.

When a suffering woman sought healing by merely touching the hem of His cloak, Jesus replied, "Be of good cheer, daughter; your faith has made you well" (Matthew 9:22 NKJV). The message to believers of every generation is clear: we must live by faith today and every day. Sometimes, however, faith is in short supply, especially when we encounter circumstances that leave us discouraged or afraid.

As Christians, we have every reason to live courageously. After all, the ultimate battle has already been fought and won on the cross at Calvary. But even dedicated followers of Christ may find their courage tested by the inevitable disappointments and fears that visit the lives of believers and non-believers alike.

The next time you find your courage tested to the limit, remember to take your fears to God. If you call upon Him, you will be comforted. Whatever your challenge, whatever your trouble, God can handle it—and will.

When you place your faith, your trust—indeed your life—in the hands of your heavenly Father, you'll be amazed at the marvelous things He can do with you and 'hrough you. So strengthen your faith through praise, worship, Bible study, and prayer. Trust God's plans. With Him, all things are possible. He stands ready to open a world of possibilities to you—*if you have faith.*

Faith in faith is pointless.
Faith in a living, active God
moves mountains.
Beth Moore

Fear is a self-imposed prison that
will keep you from becoming what
God intends for you to be.
Rick Warren

Become so wrapped up in something
that you forget to be afraid.
Lady Bird Johnson

Little faith will bring your souls
to Heaven, but great faith
will bring Heaven to your souls.
—

C. H. Spurgeon

True faith is never found alone;
it is accompanied by expectation.
C. S. *Lewis*

Faith is a strong power,
mastering any difficulty in the strength
of the Lord who made heaven and earth.
Corrie ten Boom

Prayer is the key to Heaven,
but faith unlocks the door.
Mosie Lister

Faith is two empty hands held open
to receive all of the Lord Jesus.
Alan Redpath

Faith means believing in advance
what will only make sense in reverse.
Philip Yancey

Faith in God will not get for you everything you
want, but it will get for you what God wants
you to have. The unbeliever does not need
what he wants; the Christian should
want only what he needs.
Vance Havner

No one is surprised over
what God does
when he has faith in Him.
—

Oswald Chambers

Only God can move mountains,
but faith and prayer can move God.
E. M. Bounds

Jesus said to him, "If you can believe,
all things are possible to him who believes."
Mark 9:23 NKJV

Shout the shout of faith. Nothing can
withstand the triumphant faith that links itself
to omnipotence. For "this is the victory that
overcometh the world." The secret of
all successful living lies in this shout of faith.
Hannah Whitall Smith

Blessed is the man whose strength is in You,
whose heart is set on pilgrimage.
Psalm 84:5 NKJV

Faith is the bird that sings while it is yet dark.
Anonymous

Some things have to be believed to be seen.
Ralph Hodgson

Without faith nothing is possible.
With it, nothing is impossible.
Mary McLeod Bethune

Faith is not belief without proof,
but trust without reservation.
Elton Trueblood

Faith is the belief that God will do
what is right.
Max Lucado

Have Faith and Get Busy

Here's a time-tested formula for success: have faith in God and do the work. It has been said there are no shortcuts to any place worth going. Hard work is not simply a proven way to get ahead, it's also part of God's plan for His children. God did not create us for lives of mediocrity; He created us for far greater things. Earning great things usually requires work and lots of it, which is perfectly fine with God. After all, He knows that we're up to the task, and He has big plans for us—Very big plans.

THE POWER OF OPTIMISM

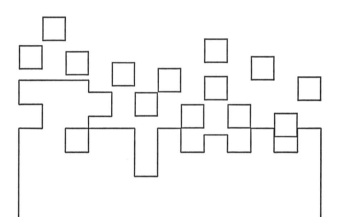

*I can do all things through Christ
who strengthens me.*
Philippians 4:13 NKJV

Are you an optimistic, hopeful, enthusiastic Christian? You should be! After all, as a believer, you have every reason to be optimistic about life here on earth and in life eternal. As C. H. Spurgeon observed, "Our hope in Christ for the future is the mainstream of our joy." But sometimes, you may find yourself pulled down by the inevitable demands and worries of everyday living. If you find yourself discouraged, exhausted, or both, it's time to take your concerns to God. When you do, He will lift your spirits and renew your strength.

Today, make this promise to yourself and keep it: vow to be a hope-filled Christian. Think optimistically about your life, your profession, your family, and your future. Trust your hopes, not your fears. Take time to celebrate God's glorious creation. Then, when you've filled your heart with hope and gladness, share your optimism with others. They'll be better for it—so will you!

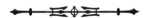

The people whom I have seen
succeed best in life have
always been cheerful
and hopeful people who went
about their business with
a smile on their faces.

—

Charles Kingsley

We can accomplish almost anything
within our ability if we but think we can.
George Matthew Adams

Talk happiness. The world is sad enough
without your woes.
Ella Wheeler Wilcox

Do you wonder where you can go
for encouragement and motivation?
Run to Jesus.
Max Lucado

The essence of optimism is that it takes no account of the present, but it is a source of inspiration, of vitality, and of hope. Where others have resigned, it enables a man to hold his head high, to claim the future for himself, and not abandon it to his enemy.

—

Dietrich Bonhoeffer

We are either the masters or the victims of
our attitudes. It is a matter of personal choice.
Who we are today is the result of choices we
made yesterday. Tomorrow, we will become
what we choose today. To change means
to choose to change.

John Maxwell

We must admit that we spend more of our
time concentrating and fretting over the
things that can't be changed than we do giving
attention to the one thing we can change:
our choice of attitude.

Charles Swindoll

The life of strain is difficult. The life of
inner peace—a life that comes from
a positive attitude—is the easiest
type of existence.

Norman Vincent Peale

Great hopes make great men.
Thomas Fuller

Make me hear joy and gladness.
Psalm 51:8 NKJV

Perpetual optimism is a force multiplier.
Colin Powell

He who believes is strong; he who doubts
is weak. Strong convictions
precede great actions.
James Freeman Clarke

Outlook determines outcome
and attitude determines action.
Warren Wiersbe

It is not fitting, when one is in God's service,
to have a gloomy face or a chilling look.
St. Francis of Assisi

When you affirm big,
believe big, and pray big,
big things happen.

—

Norman Vincent Peale

Be a Realistic Optimist

Your attitude toward the future will help create your future. So think realistically about yourself and your situation, while making a conscious effort to focus on hopes, not fears. When you do, you'll put the self-fulfilling prophecy to work *for you*.

THE POWER
OF
PERSEVERANCE

*I have fought the good fight,
I have finished the race,
I have kept the faith.*
2 Timothy 4:7 NKJV

As you continue to search for purpose in everyday life, you'll encounter your fair share of roadblocks and stumbling blocks. These situations require courage, patience, and above all, perseverance. As an example of perfect perseverance, we Christians need look no further than our Savior, Jesus Christ.

Jesus finished what He began. Despite the torture He endured, despite the shame of the cross, Jesus was steadfast in His faithfulness to God. We, too, must remain faithful, especially during times of hardship.

Perhaps you are in a hurry for God to reveal His plans for your life. If so, be forewarned: God operates on His own timetable, not yours. Sometimes, God may answer your prayers with silence. When He does, you must patiently persevere. In times of trouble, you must remain steadfast, and trust in the merciful goodness of your Heavenly Father. Whatever your problem, He can handle it. Your job is to keep persevering until He does.

*Let us run with endurance
the race that is set before us,
looking unto Jesus, the author
and finisher of our faith, who for
the joy that was set before Him
endured the cross, despising
the shame, and has sat down
at the right hand of
the throne of God.*

—

Hebrews 12:1-2 NKJV

Firmness of purpose is one of the most
necessary sinews of character, and one of
the best instruments of success.
Without it, genius wastes its effort
in a maze of inconsistencies.
Lord Chesterfield

The secret of success is constancy of purpose.
Benjamin Disraeli

All rising to a great place is by a winding stair.
Francis Bacon

By perseverance,
the snail reached the ark.
—
C. H. *Spurgeon*

Be of good courage,
And He shall strengthen
your heart, All you who hope
in the LORD.
—
Psalm 31:24 NKJV

Stand still and refuse to retreat.
Look at it as God looks at it and draw
upon his power to hold up under the blast.
Charles Swindoll

I walk slowly, but I never walk backwards.
Abraham Lincoln

Character is both developed and revealed
by tests, and all of life is a test.
Rick Warren

Take away all misfortune,
and much good would go
with it. God's care is to bring
good out of the evils
that happen,
not to abolish them.

—

Thomas Aquinas

Keep adding, keep walking, keep advancing;
do not stop, do not turn back,
do not turn from the straight road.
St. Augustine

Nothing great was ever done
without much enduring.
Catherine of Siena

Never confuse motion with action.
Ben Franklin

Nothing contributes so much to soothing
the mind as a steady purpose, a point
on which the soul may fix its intellectual eye.
Mary Wollstonecraft Shelly

Perseverance is a great element of success.
If you only knock long enough and loud
enough at the gate, you are sure
to wake up somebody.
Henry Wadsworth Longfellow

For you have need of endurance,
so that after you have done
the will of God,
you may receive the promise.
—

Hebrews 10:36 NKJV

Are You Being Tested? Call Upon God.

The next time you find your courage tested to the limit, remember God is as near as your next breath. Remember He offers strength and comfort to His children. He is your shield, your protector, and your deliverer. Call upon Him in your hour of need, and then be comforted. Whatever your challenge, whatever your trouble, God can give you the strength to persevere. That's exactly what you should ask Him to do.

ON
A PERSONAL
MISSION
FOR GOD

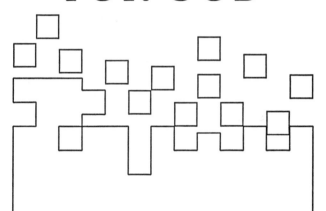

*. . . Do whatever Your hand and Your purpose
determined before to be done.*
Acts 4:28 NKJV

Whether you realize it or not, you are on a personal mission for God. As a Christian, that mission is straightforward: Honor God, accept Christ as your personal Savior, and serve God's children.

Of course, you will encounter impediments as you attempt to discover the exact nature of God's purpose for your life. But you must never lose sight of the *overriding purposes* God has established for *all* believers. You will encounter these overriding purposes again and again as you worship your Creator and study His Word.

Every day offers countless opportunities to serve God and worship Him. When you do so, He will bless you in miraculous ways. May you continue to seek God's will, may you trust His word, and may you place Him where He belongs: at the very center of your life.

You cannot walk through life without
a dream or a destination and expect to arrive
just where you wanted to go.
Lisa Bevere

I would rather die a meaningful death
than to live a meaningless life.
Corazon Aquino

Every man and woman is born into
the world to do something unique
and something distinctive, and if he or she
does not do it, it will never be done.
Benjamin Mays

Fortunate is the person who has developed
the self-control to steer a straight course
toward his objective in life, without
being swayed from his purpose by
either commendation or condemnation.
Napoleon Hill

Let us live with urgency. Let us exploit
the opportunity of life. Let us not drift.
Let us live intentionally. We must not
trifle our lives away.
Raymond Ortlund

Life is not a journey you want
to make on autopilot.
Paula Rinehart

What we are is God's gift to us.
What we become is
our gift to God.

—

Anonymous

You can have anything you want—
if you want it badly enough. You can be
anything you want to be, do anything you
set out to accomplish if you hold to
that desire with singleness of purpose.

Abraham Lincoln

The first thing each morning, and the last thing
each night, suggest to yourself specific ideas
that you wish to embody in your character
and personality. Address such suggestions to
yourself, silently or aloud, until they are
deeply impressed upon your mind.

Grenville Kleiser

This is the true joy in life: being used
for a purpose recognized by yourself
as a mighty one.

George Bernard Shaw

It is never too late
to be what
you might have been.
—

George Eliot

Be Completely Honest With Yourself

As you journey through life, you should continue to become better aquatinted with yourself. How? One way is to examine the patterns in your own life, and understand that unless you make the conscious effort to change those patterns, you're likely to repeat them. So, if you don't like some of the results you've earned, change your behaviors. The sooner you change, the sooner your results will change, too.

WORSHIPING
WITH
A PURPOSE

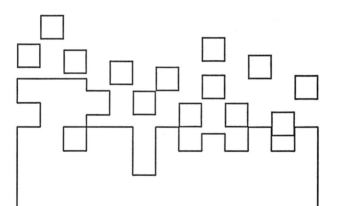

All the earth shall worship You
And sing praises to You;
They shall sing praises to Your name.
Psalm 66:4 NKJV

All of mankind is engaged in worship of one kind or another. The question is not whether we worship, but *what* we worship. Some of us choose to worship God. The result is a plentiful harvest of joy, peace, and abundance. Others distance themselves from God by foolishly worshiping things of this earth: fame, fortune, or personal gratification. To do so is a terrible mistake, with eternal consequences.

Whenever we place our love for material possessions above our love for God—or when we yield to the countless temptations of this world—we find ourselves engaged in a struggle between good and evil (a clash between God and Satan). Our responses to these struggles have implications that echo throughout our families and our communities.

How can we ensure we cast our lot with God? We do so, in part, by the practice of regular, purposeful worship in the company of fellow believers. When we worship God faithfully and fervently, we are blessed. When we fail to worship God, for whatever reason, we forfeit the spiritual gifts He intends for us.

We must worship our heavenly Father, not just with words, but also with deeds. We must honor Him, praise Him, and obey Him. As we seek to find purpose and meaning for our lives, we must first seek *His* purpose and *His* will. For believers, God comes first. Always first.

It is impossible to worship God
and remain unchanged.

—

Henry Blackaby

Spiritual worship is focusing all we are
on all He is.
Beth Moore

The deepest level of worship is praising God
in spite of pain, thanking God during a trial,
trusting him when tempted, surrendering
while suffering, and loving him when
he seems distant.
Rick Warren

Praise and thank God for who He is
and for what He has done for you.
Billy Graham

Worship is a voluntary act of gratitude offered
by the saved to the Savior, by the healed to
the Healer, by the delivered to the Deliverer.
Max Lucado

Each time, before you intercede, be quiet first
and worship God in His glory. Think of what
He can do and how He delights to hear
the prayers of His redeemed people.
Think of your place and privilege in Christ,
and expect great things!
Andrew Murray

We worship and adore You,
bowing down before You,
songs of praises singing, hallelujahs ringing.
Anonymous

The fact that we were created to
enjoy God and to worship him
forever is etched upon our souls.
Jim Cymbala

God being who He is must always be
sought for Himself, never as
a means toward something else.
A. W. Tozer

Worship is a lifestyle.
Joey Johnson

In the sanctuary,
we discover beauty:
the beauty of His presence.

—

Kay Arthur

The time for universal praise is sure
to come some day. Let us begin
to do our part now.
Hannah Whitall Smith

To praise God is to please God.
Jim Gallery

*Oh come, let us sing to the LORD!
Let us shout joyfully to the Rock of
our salvation. Let us come before
His presence with thanksgiving;
let us shout joyfully to
Him with psalms.*
Psalm 95:1-2 NKJV

Praise Him! Praise Him!
Tell of His excellent greatness.
Praise Him! Praise Him!
Ever in joyful song!
Fanny Crosby

Holy, holy, holy!
Lord God Almighty!
All Thy works shall praise Thy name
in earth, and sky, and sea.
Reginald Heber

A man can no more diminish God's glory
by refusing to worship Him than a lunatic
can put out the sun by scribbling the word
darkness on the walls of his cell.
C. S. Lewis

Worship always empowers the worshiper
with a greater revelation of
the object of her desire.
Lisa Bevere

Don't ever come to church without
coming as though it were the first time,
as though it could be the best time,
and as though it might be the last time.
Vance Havner

Sunday Morning Only or 24/7?

Worship is not meant to be boxed up in a church building on Sunday morning. To the contrary, praise and worship should be woven into the very fabric of our lives.

Do you take time each day to worship your Father in heaven? Or do you wait until Sunday morning to praise Him for His blessings? The answer to this question will, in large part, determine the quality and direction of your life. So worship accordingly.

AT PEACE
WITH
YOUR
PURPOSE

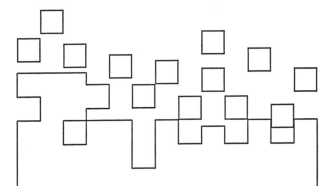

Peace I leave with you,
My peace I give to you; not as the world
gives do I give to you. Let not your heart
be troubled, neither let it be afraid.
John 14:27 NKJV

Are you at peace with the direction of your life? If you're a Christian, you should be. Perhaps you seek a new direction, or a sense of renewed purpose. Those feelings should *never* rob you of the genuine peace that can, and should be, yours through a personal relationship with Jesus. The demands of everyday living should never obscure the fact Christ died so you might have life abundant and eternal.

Have you found the lasting peace that can be yours through Jesus? Or are you still rushing after the illusion of "peace and happiness" our world promises, but cannot deliver? The beautiful words of John 14:27 remind us that Jesus offers us peace, not as the world gives, but as He alone gives. Our challenge is to accept Christ's peace into our hearts. Then, as best we can, share His peace with our neighbors.

Today, as a gift to yourself, to your family, and to your friends, claim the inner peace that is your spiritual birthright: the peace of Jesus Christ. It is offered freely; it has been paid for in full; it is yours for the asking. So ask. Then share.

That peace, which has been described
and which believers enjoy, is a participation
of the peace which their glorious Lord
and Master himself enjoys.
Jonathan Edwards

The peace that Jesus gives is never
engineered by circumstances
on the outside.
Oswald Chambers

Peace with God
is where all peace begins.

—

Jim Gallery

Peace does not mean to be in a place where
there is no noise, trouble, or hard work.
Peace means to be in the midst of all those
things and still be calm in your heart.
Catherine Marshall

Faith does not eliminate problems.
Faith keeps you in a trusting relationship
with God in the midst of your problems.
Henry Blackaby

We are not at peace with others because
we are not at peace with ourselves,
and we are not at peace with ourselves
because we are not at peace with God.
Thomas Merton

Where the Spirit of the Lord is,
there is peace;
where the Spirit of the Lord is,
there is love.

—

Stephen R. Adams

Peace within makes beauty without.
English Proverb

If there is to be any peace,
it will come through being, not having.
Henry Miller

How changed our lives would be
if we could only fly through the days
on wings of surrender and trust!
Hannah Whitall Smith

Make the least of all that goes and the most
of all that comes. Don't regret what is past.
Cherish what you have. Look forward to all
that is to come. And most important of all,
rely moment by moment on Jesus Christ.
Gigi Graham Tchividjian

And the peace of God,
which surpasses all
understanding, will guard
your hearts and minds
through Christ Jesus.
—
Philippians 4:7 NKJV

Peace is seeing a sunset
and knowing whom to thank.
—
Anonymous

Whatever It Is, God Can Handle It

Sometimes peace is a scarce commodity in a demanding, 21st century world. How can we find the peace we so desperately desire? By turning our days and our lives over to God. Elisabeth Elliot writes, "If my life is surrendered to God, all is well. Let me not grab it back, as though it were in peril in His hand but would be safer in mine!" May we give our lives, our hopes, and our prayers to the Father, and, by doing so, accept His will and His peace.

AND
FINALLY...

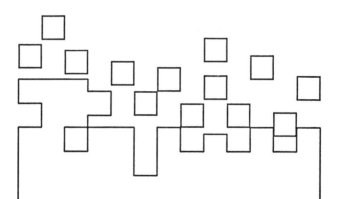

*But you are a chosen generation,
a royal priesthood, a holy nation,
His own special people, that you may
proclaim the praises of Him who called you
out of darkness into His marvelous light.*
1 Peter 2:9 NKJV

We conclude with a dozen time-tested principles for finding your purpose in everyday life. May God richly bless you as you continue on your path.

1. Remember The Search for Purpose Is a Journey, Not a Destination: Amid your changing circumstances, God will continue to reveal Himself to you, *if* you sincerely seek His will. As you journey through the stages of life, remember every new day presents fresh opportunities to seek God's will; make the conscious effort to seize those opportunities.

———

2. Pray Early and Often: Start each day with a time of prayer and devotional readings. In those quiet moments, God will lead you. Your task, of course, is to be still, to seek His will, and to follow His direction.

———

3. Quiet Please: Sometimes God speaks to you in a quiet voice. Usually, the small quiet voice inside, can help you find the right path for your life. Listen to that voice.

———

4. Use All the Tools That God Provides: As you continue to make important decisions about your future, read God's Word every day. Consult with trusted advisors whom God has seen fit to place along your path.

———

5. Take Sensible Risks in Pursuit of Personal or Professional Growth: It is better to attempt great things and fail, than to attempt nothing and succeed. But make sure to avoid *foolish* risks. When in doubt, reread Proverbs.

———

6. Expect Setbacks: Your path will have many twists and turns. When you face a setback, don't become discouraged. When you encounter a roadblock, be prepared to make a U-turn. Then, start searching for a better route to your chosen destination.

---

7. Use Your Experiences As Valued Instructors: Philosopher George Santayana correctly observed, "Those who cannot remember the past are condemned to repeat it." Act accordingly.

---

8. Write It Down: If you're facing a big decision, or if you're searching for greater fulfillment from your everyday life, begin keeping a daily journal. During quiet moments, make a written record of your thoughts, your goals, your hopes, and your concerns. The simple act of writing down your thoughts will help clarify your ideas and plans.

---

9. Don't Settle for Second, Third, or Fourth Best: God has big plans for you. Don't let Him down.

———

10. Serve Where You Stand: Even if you're not where you want to be, you can serve God exactly where you are. Don't underestimate the importance of your present work. Don't wait for a better day to serve God.

———

11. Find Pursuits About Which You Are Passionate: Find work you love and causes you believe in. You'll do your best when you become so wrapped up in something, that you forget to call it work.

———

12. Have Faith and Get Busy: Remember the words of Cyrus Curtis: "Believe in the Lord and He will do half the work—the last half."

And Finally, a Few Thoughts About Purpose

Make your life a mission—not an intermission.
Arnold H. Glasgow

The purpose of life is a life of purpose.
Robert Byrne

The man without a purpose is like a ship
without a rudder: a waif, a nothing, a no man.
Have a purpose in life and having it,
throw strength of mind and muscle
into your work.
Thomas Carlyle

As a well-spent day brings happy sleep,
so a life we used brings happy death.
Leonardo da Vinci

Great minds have purposes;
others have wishes.
Washington Irving

The great and glorious masterpiece of
man is how to live with a purpose.
Michel de Montaigne

Make each day your masterpiece.
John Wooden

No steam or river ever drives anything until it is confined. No Niagara is ever turned into light and power until it is harnessed. No life ever grows until it is focused, dedicated, disciplined.

—

Harry Emerson Fosdick

Teach me Your way, O LORD;
I will walk in Your truth.

—

Psalm 86:11 NKJV

*Trust in the L*ORD *with all
your heart, and lean not on your
own understanding;
In all your ways acknowledge
Him, And He shall
direct your paths.*

—

Proverbs 3:5–6 NKJV

About Criswell Freeman

Criswell Freeman's books have sold millions of copies, yet his name is largely *unknown* to the general public. *The Wall Street Journal* observed, "Normally, a tally like that would put a writer on the best-seller lists. But Freeman is hardly a household name." And that's exactly how the author likes it.

The Washington Post called Freeman "possibly the most prolific 'quote book' writer in America." With little fanfare, Dr. Freeman has compiled and edited well over a hundred titles that have now sold over 8,000,000 copies.

Freeman began his writing career as a self-help author (his first book was entitled *When Life Throws You a Curveball, Hit It*). Today, Freeman's writings focus on the Good News of God's Holy Word. Criswell is a Doctor of Clinical Psychology (he earned his degree from the Adler School of Professional Psychology in Chicago). He earned his undergraduate degree at Vanderbilt University. Freeman also attended classes at The Southern Baptist Theological Seminary in Louisville where he studied under the noted pastoral counselor Wayne Oates.

Criswell lives in Nashville, Tennessee. He is married and has two daughters.